Emotional Intelligence in Business: Strategies for Entrepreneurs to Lead with Empathy, Resilience, and Innovation

Ellen M. Brooks

In today's fast-paced business world, emotional intelligence is no longer optional—it's essential. The ability to understand and manage emotions, both yours and others', sets successful leaders apart. Emotional Intelligence in Business offers practical strategies to help you develop this vital skill, empowering you to lead with empathy, make better decisions, and build stronger teams.

This book is your guide to mastering emotional intelligence and transforming it into your most valuable business asset.

Contents

Why Emotional Intelligence is the Competitive Edge in Business Today — 1

Self-Awareness and Emotional Regulation: Mastering Yourself as an Entrepreneur — 4

Empathy in Leadership: Building Trust and Enhancing Team Dynamics — 8

Emotional Intelligence in Decision-Making: Data Meets Intuition — 12

Building Resilience Through Emotional Intelligence: Staying Strong in the Face of Challenges — 18

Leading with Empathy: Emotional Intelligence in Team Building and Leadership — 24

Emotional Intelligence in Decision-Making: How to Make Smarter, More Informed Choices — 31

Conflict Resolution with Emotional Intelligence — 37

Building Resilience Through Emotional Intelligence — 43

Emotional Agility: Adapting Quickly to Change and Uncertainty — 49

Leading Teams Through Organizational Change — 56

The Future of Emotional Intelligence in Business: Trends and Predictions — 63

Chapter 1: Why Emotional Intelligence is the Competitive Edge in Business Today

In today's fast-moving business landscape, where change is constant and competition is fierce, technical skills and business acumen alone are no longer enough. To truly excel, entrepreneurs need an advantage that goes beyond traditional intelligence and expertise: they need emotional intelligence (EI). Emotional intelligence is quickly becoming the hallmark of the most successful business leaders, shaping the way they interact with their teams, make decisions, and innovate.

The Power of Emotional Intelligence in Business

Research has consistently shown that emotionally intelligent leaders outperform their peers in various dimensions of business, from employee engagement to customer satisfaction and financial performance. A landmark study by TalentSmart found that 90% of top performers possess high emotional intelligence, while 80% of low performers struggle with low EI.

In a business context, emotional intelligence isn't just about managing emotions—it's about using emotional awareness as a tool for better leadership, innovation, and decision-making. Entrepreneurs who develop high emotional intelligence can create stronger bonds with their teams, foster collaboration, and lead with empathy. This, in turn, leads to better outcomes in high-stakes negotiations, product development, and even customer relations.

Why Emotional Intelligence Matters More Than Ever

The modern business environment is more dynamic and unpredictable than ever before. From the rise of remote work to rapidly evolving customer expectations, entrepreneurs today face challenges that require agility, resilience, and strong interpersonal skills. The COVID-19 pandemic showed us just how important it is for leaders to manage their own emotions and those of their teams in times of uncertainty and stress.

Emotional intelligence gives entrepreneurs the ability to adapt quickly to changing circumstances, navigate complex social dynamics, and maintain a positive, resilient mindset even in the face of adversity. It enables leaders to maintain clarity under pressure and to make decisions that are both emotionally and strategically sound.

Case Studies of Successful Entrepreneurs Using EI
Consider the case of Jeff Weiner, the former CEO of LinkedIn. Weiner transformed LinkedIn into a multi-billion-dollar company by emphasizing the importance of compassionate leadership. Weiner made emotional intelligence a central part of LinkedIn's culture, focusing on leading with empathy and compassion in all areas of business—from managing employees to dealing with customers and investors.

Similarly, Arianna Huffington, founder of the Huffington Post and Thrive Global, has become a vocal advocate for emotional intelligence, particularly the importance of managing stress and burnout. Huffington often discusses how self-awareness and emotional regulation have helped her build her businesses and maintain her personal well-being, showing that emotional intelligence isn't just a business tool—it's a life skill.
In both cases, these leaders demonstrate how emotional intelligence is a key differentiator in leadership and entrepreneurship. It allows entrepreneurs to build stronger, more resilient teams, navigate crises with confidence, and foster innovation in their companies.

The Competitive Edge
In a world where technical skills are abundant, emotional intelligence is the competitive edge that can set entrepreneurs apart. Leaders who develop high EI are not only better equipped to manage their teams but also to understand the emotional needs of their customers and partners. Emotional intelligence helps entrepreneurs build relationships, negotiate effectively, and lead with authenticity—all crucial traits for long-term success in business.

As the business landscape continues to evolve, emotional intelligence will play an even bigger role in determining who thrives and who struggles to keep up. Entrepreneurs who invest in their emotional intelligence are investing in their future success. By mastering self-awareness, empathy, emotional regulation, and social intelligence, today's entrepreneurs can build businesses that are not only profitable but also resilient, innovative, and adaptive to change.

Chapter 2: Self-Awareness and Emotional Regulation: Mastering Yourself as an Entrepreneur

Success in entrepreneurship is often attributed to ambition, creativity, and resilience. However, a less visible but equally crucial trait is the ability to regulate emotions and maintain an acute sense of self-awareness. These qualities allow entrepreneurs to make decisions with clarity, remain calm under pressure, and stay connected to their deeper purpose. In this chapter, we'll dive into the science behind self-awareness and emotional regulation and explore advanced techniques that can help entrepreneurs gain a competitive edge.

The Science of Self-Awareness: Understanding the "Why" Behind Your Emotions

At its core, self-awareness is the ability to recognize and understand your own emotions and how they influence your thoughts, behaviors, and decisions. Neuroscientists often refer to this as the ability to create a "meta-awareness" of your emotional states, where you can observe your emotions without being overwhelmed by them.

Daniel Goleman, the psychologist who popularized emotional intelligence, identifies self-awareness as the foundation of EI. Entrepreneurs with strong self-awareness can understand their emotional triggers, motivations, and how their mood influences their decision-making processes. This awareness allows them to step back and assess situations more objectively, especially in high-stakes moments.

Recent studies in neuroscience show that the prefrontal cortex, the part of the brain responsible for decision-making and self-control, plays a critical role in self-awareness. Mindfulness practices, for example, have been proven to strengthen the prefrontal cortex, enhancing self-awareness and improving emotional regulation. Entrepreneurs who cultivate these abilities are better equipped to make clear-headed decisions, even under stress.

Practical Techniques to Build Self-Awareness
Building self-awareness doesn't happen overnight, but there are practical strategies entrepreneurs can implement to start sharpening this skill:

1. Daily Reflection: Take time each day to reflect on your emotional responses to different situations. Journaling about decisions, team interactions, or moments of stress can help you identify patterns in your emotional triggers and reactions.

2. Mindfulness Meditation: Meditation is a powerful tool for enhancing self-awareness. Studies show that regular meditation can improve focus, emotional regulation, and the ability to observe emotions without reacting impulsively. By spending even 10 minutes a day in mindfulness practice, entrepreneurs can train their brains to be more emotionally aware.

3. Seeking Feedback: Often, our blind spots can only be seen by others. Seeking feedback from trusted colleagues, mentors, or coaches can give entrepreneurs an outside perspective on their emotional habits and behaviors. Feedback provides an opportunity to learn how others perceive your leadership style and emotional responses, further enhancing self-awareness.

By understanding these emotional patterns, entrepreneurs can make better decisions, lead with authenticity, and stay aligned with their values in challenging situations.

Emotional Regulation: The Key to Consistent Leadership
Once self-awareness is developed, the next step is learning how to regulate emotions effectively. Emotional regulation doesn't mean suppressing or ignoring emotions but rather managing them in a way that enhances performance and decision-making.

For entrepreneurs, the ability to regulate emotions is crucial in moments of high stress or when quick decisions need to be made. The best leaders are those who can maintain their composure in the face of adversity, remaining calm and clear-headed while others may falter.

The Neuroscience of Emotional Regulation
Neuroscience research shows that emotional regulation is largely governed by the interaction between the prefrontal cortex and the amygdala, the part of the brain responsible for processing emotions like fear and anxiety. When entrepreneurs are faced with stressful situations, the amygdala can trigger a "fight or flight" response, leading to impulsive decisions or emotional outbursts. However, with practice, entrepreneurs can train their prefrontal cortex to override these reactions and maintain control.

One technique that has gained attention for its effectiveness in emotional regulation is cognitive reappraisal. This involves consciously reinterpreting a stressful situation to change its emotional impact. For example, instead of viewing a business setback as a failure, an entrepreneur might reframe it as a learning opportunity, allowing them to stay motivated and focused.

Advanced Emotional Regulation Techniques
Entrepreneurs can benefit from mastering a few advanced emotional regulation strategies:

1.Cognitive Reappraisal: As mentioned above, cognitive reappraisal is one of the most effective strategies for regulating emotions. It allows entrepreneurs to change their emotional response to a situation by shifting their perspective. For instance, if a meeting doesn't go as planned, instead of dwelling on frustration, you could focus on what you've learned and how to improve for the next meeting.

2.Breathing Exercises: Deep, controlled breathing is a simple but powerful tool for managing emotions in stressful situations. By slowing down your breath, you activate your body's parasympathetic nervous system, which helps to calm the mind and reduce feelings of anxiety or anger. A common technique is box breathing: inhale for four seconds, hold for four seconds, exhale for four seconds, and hold again for four seconds.

3.Taking a Pause Before Reacting: One hallmark of emotional intelligence is the ability to pause before responding emotionally to a situation. In moments of high stress, it's easy to react impulsively. However, by training yourself to take a brief pause—whether it's 10 seconds or a minute—you give your brain time to process the emotion and respond more thoughtfully. This can prevent rash decisions or emotional outbursts.

4.Physical Activity: Physical exercise is another proven way to regulate emotions. Studies show that aerobic exercise, in particular, reduces anxiety, improves mood, and increases the brain's ability to handle stress. Entrepreneurs who incorporate regular physical activity into their routine are better able to handle emotional challenges in the workplace.

Mastering Yourself as an Entrepreneur
At the end of the day, self-awareness and emotional regulation are not just tools for managing stress—they are critical components of successful entrepreneurship. Entrepreneurs who know themselves deeply, who can manage their emotions under pressure, and who have the resilience to keep going when things get tough, are the ones who lead their teams to victory.

Mastering yourself as an entrepreneur means embracing the continuous process of self-awareness, reflection, and emotional regulation. The journey may not always be easy, but the rewards are immense: clearer decision-making, stronger relationships, and a more grounded approach to leadership. These are the qualities that set great entrepreneurs apart from the rest.

Chapter 3: Empathy in Leadership: Building Trust and Enhancing Team Dynamics

Empathy, often defined as the ability to understand and share the feelings of others, is not just a soft skill reserved for personal relationships—it's a powerful leadership tool. In business, empathy is crucial for building trust, improving communication, and enhancing team performance. Entrepreneurs who lead with empathy create work environments where employees feel valued and understood, leading to higher levels of engagement and productivity.

In this chapter, we'll explore the role of empathy in leadership, discuss its impact on team dynamics, and offer strategies for entrepreneurs to incorporate empathy into their daily interactions with employees, partners, and customers.

The Science of Empathy in Leadership
Empathy is one of the key components of emotional intelligence and plays a significant role in how leaders connect with their teams. Neuroscientific research shows that empathy is hardwired into our brains—humans are naturally inclined to connect with others and understand their emotional states through mirror neurons, which activate when we observe someone else's emotions or actions.

However, in the fast-paced world of entrepreneurship, empathy can sometimes be overlooked in favor of efficiency or performance. The truth is, empathy enhances both performance and efficiency by creating an atmosphere where people feel safe to share ideas, voice concerns, and work collaboratively without fear of judgment.

Recent studies also highlight that empathetic leadership leads to increased employee retention, loyalty, and job satisfaction. In a survey by Businessolver, 93% of employees said they are more likely to stay with an empathetic employer, and 82% of employees would consider leaving their job for a more empathetic organization. This underscores the competitive advantage entrepreneurs gain when they lead with empathy.

Recent studies also highlight that empathetic leadership leads to increased employee retention, loyalty, and job satisfaction. In a survey by Businessolver, 93% of employees said they are more likely to stay with an empathetic employer, and 82% of employees would consider leaving their job for a more empathetic organization. This underscores the competitive advantage entrepreneurs gain when they lead with empathy.

Building Trust Through Empathy
Trust is the foundation of any successful relationship, and in business, it's critical for team cohesion and performance. When employees trust their leader, they are more likely to stay motivated, take risks, and go above and beyond for the business. Empathy is the key to building that trust.

When leaders show empathy, they demonstrate that they are not only concerned with results but also with the well-being of their team members. This creates a sense of psychological safety, which research has shown is one of the most important factors in high-performing teams. Employees are more likely to share innovative ideas and take risks when they trust their leader to support them, even in failure.

Empathy also helps leaders better understand the needs and motivations of their employees. For example, an empathetic leader might recognize that a team member is struggling due to personal stress and offer flexibility or support. By showing that they care about the individual behind the job title, entrepreneurs can foster deeper loyalty and commitment from their team.

Practical Strategies for Leading with Empathy
Empathy may come naturally to some leaders, but for others, it is a skill that can be developed with intention. Here are practical strategies for entrepreneurs to cultivate empathy in their leadership style:

- Active Listening: One of the most powerful ways to demonstrate empathy is through active listening. This means giving your full attention to the person speaking, acknowledging their emotions, and responding thoughtfully.

- Understanding Non-Verbal Cues: Empathy often involves interpreting unspoken emotions, which are communicated through body language, facial expressions, and tone of voice. Being attuned to these cues can help you understand how someone is feeling even if they don't explicitly say it.

Tip: Pay attention to subtle changes in body language, such as crossed arms, fidgeting, or changes in tone, as these can provide insight into how someone is really feeling.

- Personal Check-Ins: Make it a habit to check in with team members on a personal level, not just about their work but also about how they're doing overall. This shows that you care about them as individuals, not just as employees.

Tip: A simple, "How are you doing, really?" can open the door for more meaningful conversations and provide you with the opportunity to offer support where needed.

- Empathy in Decision-Making: When making decisions that affect your team, consider the emotional impact of your choices. Empathetic leaders weigh not only the financial and operational outcomes but also how changes will affect their people.

Tip: Before implementing a new policy or making a big decision, ask yourself how it will impact the people involved. Consider seeking input from your team to understand their perspectives.

- Creating a Culture of Empathy: Empathy should not just be a top-down trait; it needs to permeate the entire organization. Encourage a culture where team members practice empathy with one another. This can be done through open communication, collaborative projects, and recognizing empathetic behavior in others.

Tip: Implement team-building exercises that emphasize understanding and collaboration, and make empathy a core value in your company culture.

The Role of Empathy in Conflict Resolution
Conflict is inevitable in any business setting, but empathetic leaders are better equipped to navigate these challenges. Empathy allows leaders to understand the emotions and perspectives of both sides in a conflict, which is essential for resolving issues in a way that feels fair to all parties involved.

For example, if two team members are clashing over a project, an empathetic leader would take the time to listen to each person's concerns and emotions, rather than simply focusing on the surface-level disagreement. By acknowledging the feelings and motivations driving the conflict, leaders can find solutions that address the root of the issue and help prevent future misunderstandings.

Empathy in conflict resolution also means approaching disagreements with a mindset of collaboration rather than competition. When leaders show that they care about finding a resolution that benefits everyone, it fosters a more cooperative atmosphere, and team members are more likely to work together to solve problems.

Chapter 4: Emotional Intelligence in Decision-Making: Data Meets Intuition

In today's business landscape, data is often hailed as the ultimate decision-making tool. Numbers, metrics, and analytics can provide invaluable insights, but data alone is not enough to guarantee success. Some of the most effective business decisions come from a fusion of data-driven strategies and emotional intelligence (EI). Emotional intelligence allows entrepreneurs to understand the human elements behind the numbers, helping them make more informed, empathetic, and intuitive decisions.

In this chapter, we'll explore how EI and data-driven decision-making can work together, giving entrepreneurs the tools to navigate uncertainty, understand their customers and teams better, and make smarter business choices.

The Limitations of Data-Only Decision-Making
Data is often presented as the "objective truth" in decision-making, but even the most comprehensive data has its limitations. It's critical for entrepreneurs to recognize these limitations and understand when emotional intelligence should complement data analysis.

- Context and Human Emotion: Data can tell you what happened, but it often lacks the nuance to explain why. For example, sales figures may show a dip in performance, but the data won't explain the emotional state of the sales team or whether customers were dissatisfied for emotional or experiential reasons. This is where EI comes in: by understanding the emotions and motivations behind the numbers, entrepreneurs can make more holistic decisions.

- Bias in Data Interpretation: Despite being seen as objective, data can be subject to bias based on how it is collected, interpreted, and presented. For example, over-reliance on certain metrics may cause decision-makers to miss underlying trends that could be critical to long-term success. Emotional intelligence helps leaders challenge these biases by encouraging them to take a broader view, including the emotional and psychological factors that influence customer and employee behavior.
- The Risk of Analysis Paralysis: With the explosion of big data, entrepreneurs often face the challenge of "analysis paralysis"—getting bogged down by too much information, leading to delayed or indecisive actions. Emotional intelligence allows leaders to trust their instincts and balance data with intuition, helping them act with confidence even when the data isn't 100% conclusive.

The Power of Intuition in Business

Intuition, often referred to as a "gut feeling," is the product of our brain's ability to synthesize vast amounts of information, including past experiences, knowledge, and emotional cues, into a coherent sense of what feels right. While intuition may not always be measurable, it plays a vital role in decision-making, particularly when dealing with uncertainty or incomplete data.

Neuroscience has shown that intuition is not a mystical ability but rather the brain's way of processing patterns and signals that the conscious mind might not immediately recognize. Emotional intelligence sharpens this intuition, allowing entrepreneurs to tap into their subconscious understanding of situations, making them better at reading between the lines.

Case Study: Steve Jobs and Intuition

One of the most famous proponents of intuition in business was Steve Jobs, the co-founder of Apple. Jobs often spoke about how he relied on his intuition when making critical business decisions. He famously ignored traditional market research when designing the iPhone, trusting instead in his ability to anticipate customer desires and emotional responses to the product. The success of the iPhone is a testament to how intuition, guided by emotional intelligence, can lead to groundbreaking innovation.

Balancing Data with Emotional Intelligence: A Practical Framework
Entrepreneurs don't have to choose between data and emotional intelligence—they can use both to create a more balanced approach to decision-making. Here's a practical framework for integrating EI into data-driven decisions:

- Start with the Data: Begin by analyzing the data available. Look for trends, patterns, and actionable insights. But remember, data provides the "what" and not always the "why." Use this as your foundation, but be ready to dig deeper.
- Apply Empathy and Perspective-Taking: Once you have the data, ask yourself how it aligns with the emotional experiences of your team, customers, or stakeholders. For instance, if customer churn is increasing, what emotional factors might be driving this? Could there be frustration with customer service, dissatisfaction with the product's user experience, or a loss of trust in the brand? Empathy allows you to interpret the data in a more human context.
- Consider the Human Element: As you make decisions based on the data, consider the potential emotional impact on your team and customers. Will a decision improve team morale, or will it create friction? Will it increase customer loyalty, or could it alienate a key demographic? Balancing these emotional factors with the raw data leads to more well-rounded decisions.
- Leverage Cognitive Reappraisal: This emotional intelligence tool (discussed in Chapter 2) can be applied to decision-making. When faced with negative data or challenges, use cognitive reappraisal to shift your perspective. Instead of viewing poor sales as a failure, reframe it as an opportunity to innovate or improve. This mindset can help entrepreneurs stay resilient and positive in the face of setbacks.

- Leverage Cognitive Reappraisal: This emotional intelligence tool (discussed in Chapter 2) can be applied to decision-making. When faced with negative data or challenges, use cognitive reappraisal to shift your perspective. Instead of viewing poor sales as a failure, reframe it as an opportunity to innovate or improve. This mindset can help entrepreneurs stay resilient and positive in the face of setbacks.
- Trust Your Instincts: After weighing the data and emotional insights, trust your gut. Emotional intelligence allows you to process complex information on a subconscious level. When the data is inconclusive or conflicting, don't be afraid to follow your intuition, especially if it aligns with your past experiences and the emotional pulse of your business.

Case Studies: Data Meets Emotional Intelligence in Action

Let's look at some examples of how combining data with emotional intelligence has led to business success.

Amazon's Customer-Centric Approach

Amazon is known for its data-driven culture, but its success also stems from an empathetic understanding of customer needs. Under Jeff Bezos' leadership, Amazon has always prioritized customer satisfaction above all else. While data helps Amazon optimize its logistics and offerings, its emotional intelligence—understanding customers' frustrations and desires—has been key in creating services like Amazon Prime and one-click purchasing. By blending data with empathy, Amazon has fostered intense customer loyalty.

Netflix's Emotional Engagement Strategy

Netflix uses extensive data analytics to recommend shows and predict viewing trends, but the company's success also lies in its emotional intelligence. Netflix understands how customers emotionally engage with content. It tracks data not just on what people watch, but on how they watch—do they binge-watch certain shows, pause frequently, or skip episodes?

This data is combined with an understanding of emotional drivers, leading to original content that resonates deeply with audiences. Shows like Stranger Things or The Crown are successful because they tap into viewers' emotions, creating a loyal fanbase.

Emotional Intelligence in Risk-Taking and Innovation
Entrepreneurs often face situations where they need to take calculated risks. In these moments, data can offer valuable insights, but emotional intelligence provides the courage and insight to move forward when the data is incomplete or inconclusive.

For example, in the early stages of a startup, data on market potential might be limited, but entrepreneurs with high EI can intuit customer needs based on personal experience or emotional observation. By staying attuned to the emotional responses of potential customers, entrepreneurs can launch products that resonate emotionally, even in uncertain markets.

Additionally, emotional intelligence helps leaders handle the emotional risk involved in innovation. Innovative ideas are often met with resistance, both internally and externally. Entrepreneurs with strong emotional intelligence can navigate the skepticism, maintain their conviction, and continue moving forward even when the data suggests uncertainty.

The Long-Term Impact of Emotionally Intelligent Decision-Making
In the long term, emotionally intelligent decision-making builds stronger relationships with customers, employees, and partners. Leaders who combine data with empathy are better able to anticipate the needs of their stakeholders, leading to greater customer loyalty and employee retention.
Moreover, emotionally intelligent leaders are more resilient in the face of challenges. They can adapt to changing circumstances by balancing analytical insights with an intuitive understanding of the human factors at play. This adaptability is critical in today's fast-paced, constantly evolving business landscape.

Conclusion: Merging Data and Emotion for Success
Entrepreneurs who master the balance between data-driven analysis and emotional intelligence will gain a significant competitive advantage. Data provides valuable insights, but emotional intelligence adds depth, allowing leaders to interpret data through a human lens and make decisions that resonate on an emotional level.

Incorporating emotional intelligence into decision-making doesn't mean ignoring the data—it means recognizing that emotions drive behavior, and understanding those emotions can help entrepreneurs make better, more informed decisions. The most successful business leaders are those who use both their heads and their hearts, combining the precision of data with the wisdom of emotional insight.

Chapter 5: Building Resilience Through Emotional Intelligence: Staying Strong in the Face of Challenges

Every entrepreneur faces setbacks, challenges, and moments of uncertainty. The ability to stay resilient in the face of adversity is one of the most crucial traits for long-term success. Resilience is not just about "toughing it out"—it involves emotional flexibility, self-awareness, and adaptability. These qualities are all integral parts of emotional intelligence (EI).

In this chapter, we'll explore how entrepreneurs can use emotional intelligence to build resilience, manage stress, and maintain their focus and energy during tough times. By mastering EI, business leaders can bounce back from challenges more effectively, make better decisions under pressure, and maintain their mental and emotional well-being.

Understanding Resilience: More Than Just Perseverance
Resilience is often misunderstood as sheer perseverance, but in reality, it's about much more than pushing through difficulties. True resilience involves the ability to recover quickly from setbacks, adapt to change, and continue moving forward with purpose. Emotionally intelligent resilience combines:

- Emotional Regulation: The ability to manage negative emotions (like frustration, anger, or disappointment) and channel them in productive ways.
- Cognitive Flexibility: The capacity to adapt your thinking in response to new challenges, pivot strategies, and find creative solutions.
- Optimism and Reframing: Maintaining a positive outlook and reframing challenges as opportunities for growth rather than failures.

Recent psychological research shows that resilient people tend to be more emotionally intelligent—they're better able to process and regulate their emotions, which allows them to navigate stress more effectively and recover from setbacks with a healthier mindset.

Emotional Intelligence as the Foundation for Resilience

Emotional intelligence provides the tools needed to build resilience, especially in high-pressure entrepreneurial environments. Let's explore the specific components of EI that support resilience.

Self-Awareness: Self-awareness is the foundation of both emotional intelligence and resilience. When entrepreneurs are self-aware, they can recognize their own emotional triggers and reactions during stressful times. By understanding these internal responses, they can better manage their emotions and avoid being overwhelmed by them.
- Tip: Practice mindfulness to enhance self-awareness. Regularly check in with yourself to notice how you're feeling emotionally and physically, especially when stress levels rise. This self-check can help you intervene early and manage your reactions before they spiral out of control.

Self-Regulation: Self-regulation is the ability to manage your emotions in a healthy and constructive way. In moments of stress, resilient entrepreneurs don't let frustration, fear, or anger cloud their judgment. Instead, they pause, assess their emotional state, and choose a response that aligns with their goals.
- Tip: Use techniques like deep breathing, taking breaks, or reframing negative thoughts to help regulate emotions in the heat of the moment. Self-regulation isn't about suppressing emotions—it's about acknowledging them without letting them dictate your actions.

Empathy: Empathy not only helps entrepreneurs connect with others but also enables them to better understand and manage their own emotional responses. When challenges arise, empathy allows leaders to put themselves in the shoes of their employees, partners, and customers, creating a broader perspective on the situation.
- Tip: During times of crisis, take a moment to consider how others around you might be feeling. Empathy can help reduce stress by fostering understanding and cooperation within your team, turning difficult situations into collaborative problem-solving opportunities.

Motivation: Resilient entrepreneurs are driven by an internal sense of purpose and motivation. This intrinsic motivation helps them stay focused on their long-term goals, even in the face of temporary setbacks. Emotional intelligence amplifies this by helping leaders connect their daily actions with their deeper motivations, making it easier to push through challenges.
- Tip: When facing obstacles, reconnect with your "why." Reflect on why you started your business and what drives your passion. Keeping your ultimate vision in mind can help you stay motivated and resilient during tough times.

Social Skills and Support Systems: Emotional intelligence enhances social skills, allowing entrepreneurs to build strong support systems. Resilience isn't a solo endeavor; it often depends on the relationships and networks you've cultivated. Entrepreneurs with high EI know when to seek support, collaborate with others, and rely on their team during difficult periods.
- Tip: Don't be afraid to lean on your support network during times of stress. Whether it's colleagues, mentors, friends, or family, having people to talk to can help relieve pressure and offer new perspectives on challenges.

Using Emotional Intelligence to Manage Stress

Stress is an inevitable part of entrepreneurship, but how you manage that stress makes all the difference. Emotional intelligence equips entrepreneurs with the tools to handle stress in a healthier, more effective way.

Cognitive Reappraisal: One of the most powerful EI techniques for managing stress is cognitive reappraisal, which involves changing the way you think about stressful situations. Instead of seeing a challenge as a threat, you can reframe it as an opportunity for learning or growth.
- Example: If a project fails, instead of viewing it as a personal or business failure, see it as a chance to analyze what went wrong, learn from the experience, and implement new strategies for success. This shift in perspective helps reduce stress and fosters a growth mindset.

Building Emotional Agility: Emotional agility is the ability to stay flexible and adapt your emotional responses as circumstances change. Entrepreneurs with high emotional agility can quickly shift from frustration to problem-solving mode, allowing them to recover faster from setbacks.
- Tip: When you feel stuck in a negative emotional loop, practice "naming and detaching" from your emotions. By labeling what you're feeling (e.g., "I'm feeling anxious about this deadline"), you can create some mental distance, which makes it easier to move forward with action rather than dwelling on the emotion.

Positive Psychology and Gratitude: Research in positive psychology has shown that practices like gratitude and optimism can significantly improve resilience and reduce stress. Emotionally intelligent entrepreneurs make it a habit to focus on the positive aspects of their situation, even during difficult times.
- Tip: Keep a gratitude journal or take a few moments each day to reflect on what's going well. Focusing on the positive helps shift your mindset from scarcity to abundance, making it easier to stay resilient in the face of challenges.

Developing a Growth Mindset Through Emotional Intelligence

A growth mindset, as popularized by psychologist Carol Dweck, is the belief that abilities and intelligence can be developed through dedication and hard work. Entrepreneurs with a growth mindset are more resilient because they see challenges as opportunities to grow rather than insurmountable obstacles.

Emotional intelligence fosters a growth mindset by helping leaders remain open to learning, embrace feedback, and stay curious. Instead of feeling threatened by failure, emotionally intelligent entrepreneurs use setbacks as fuel for personal and business growth.

- Example: Sara Blakely, the founder of Spanx, famously talks about how her father would ask her, "What did you fail at today?" at the dinner table. This question was meant to normalize failure and frame it as a learning experience. Blakely attributes much of her success to this early encouragement to view setbacks as opportunities for growth.

Resilience in Action: Leading Through Crisis
Let's look at how emotional intelligence and resilience play out in real-world business crises.

The Airbnb Story: In the early days of Airbnb, the founders struggled to gain traction and nearly went bankrupt multiple times. However, their resilience and emotional intelligence helped them pivot their strategy and ultimately succeed. Co-founder Brian Chesky has spoken about how they had to learn from customer feedback, remain adaptable, and keep their vision alive even when things looked bleak. Their ability to stay resilient, manage stress, and maintain motivation through difficult times is a testament to the power of emotional intelligence in entrepreneurship.

Howard Schultz and Starbucks' Turnaround: In 2008, Howard Schultz returned as CEO of Starbucks during a major financial downturn. Schultz faced enormous pressure to cut costs, but instead, he focused on restoring the company's culture and connection with its employees and customers. His emotionally intelligent leadership during this crisis involved listening to the concerns of employees, building trust, and showing empathy, all while keeping a clear vision of the company's values. By leading with resilience and emotional intelligence, Schultz was able to steer Starbucks back to profitability.

Cultivating Long-Term Resilience: Daily Practices
Building emotional resilience doesn't happen overnight—it's something that entrepreneurs need to cultivate through regular practices and habits. Here are a few daily strategies to help develop long-term resilience through emotional intelligence:

1. Daily Reflection: Take time each day to reflect on your emotional state, challenges, and successes. This practice helps build self-awareness and prepares you to manage emotions more effectively.
2. Mindfulness and Meditation: Regular mindfulness practices help you stay grounded, reduce stress, and enhance your ability to respond to challenges with calm and clarity.
3. Physical Well-being: Resilience is closely tied to physical health. Prioritize exercise, sleep, and nutrition, as they all play a role in managing stress and staying emotionally balanced.
4. Continuous Learning: Keep challenging yourself to learn new skills, take on new challenges, and expand your emotional intelligence. The more you grow, the more resilient you become in the face of adversity.

Conclusion: The Power of Resilient Leadership
Building resilience through emotional intelligence is essential for long-term success as an entrepreneur. By mastering emotional regulation, maintaining a positive outlook, and leveraging support systems, emotionally intelligent leaders can not only survive but thrive in the face of challenges.

Resilience is not about avoiding stress or difficulty—it's about learning how to bounce back stronger. Entrepreneurs who cultivate emotional intelligence build a foundation of resilience that allows them to navigate uncertainty, stay adaptable, and continue driving their businesses forward, no matter what obstacles arise.

Chapter 6: Leading with Empathy: Emotional Intelligence in Team Building and Leadership

One of the most powerful ways to lead a team is through empathy. Empathy, a cornerstone of emotional intelligence (EI), allows leaders to connect with their teams on a deeper level, understand their needs, and create an environment where everyone feels valued and heard. In today's rapidly changing business environment, leaders who prioritize empathy are better equipped to build strong, resilient teams that can navigate uncertainty and stay motivated through challenges.

This chapter explores how emotionally intelligent leadership, particularly empathy, plays a critical role in team building, enhancing productivity, and fostering a positive and collaborative company culture.

The Importance of Empathy in Leadership
Empathy in leadership is about understanding and sharing the feelings of others—whether it's an employee struggling with a personal issue, a team member feeling frustrated by a challenging project, or an entire team facing burnout. While some leaders may see empathy as "soft" or secondary to business goals, research increasingly shows that empathy directly impacts team performance, engagement, and overall company success.

Empathy Enhances Employee Engagement: Teams led by empathetic leaders tend to have higher levels of engagement. When employees feel that their leaders truly care about their well-being and understand their challenges, they are more likely to be committed to their work and the organization. This leads to higher productivity, better job satisfaction, and lower turnover.

Empathy Improves Communication: Effective communication is central to any successful team, and empathy enhances communication by fostering an environment where people feel comfortable sharing their thoughts, concerns, and ideas. When leaders listen empathetically, they create a safe space for honest dialogue, which in turn improves decision-making and problem-solving within the team.

Empathy Builds Trust: Trust is the foundation of any successful team, and empathy is key to building and maintaining trust. Leaders who demonstrate empathy show their teams that they are genuinely interested in their success and well-being. This creates a sense of psychological safety, where team members feel they can take risks, make mistakes, and innovate without fear of judgment or repercussions.

Empathy Promotes Collaboration: Empathy encourages collaboration by helping team members feel understood and valued. When leaders model empathy, they inspire a culture of mutual respect, where team members are more willing to support each other and work together towards shared goals. Empathy helps break down silos and fosters a spirit of teamwork.

How Emotional Intelligence Improves Team Dynamics

Emotional intelligence goes beyond empathy, encompassing self-awareness, self-regulation, motivation, and social skills—all of which are critical for effective leadership. Here's how EI improves team dynamics:

Self-Awareness in Leadership: Self-aware leaders understand their own emotions, strengths, and weaknesses, which allows them to lead with authenticity and confidence. This self-awareness also helps leaders recognize how their emotions and behaviors impact the team. For example, a leader who is aware of their tendency to become impatient under stress can take steps to manage their reactions and avoid creating unnecessary tension within the team.
- Tip: Regular self-reflection and seeking feedback from your team can help improve self-awareness. Being open about your own challenges and areas for growth models vulnerability, which can build stronger relationships with your team.

Self-Regulation and Emotional Stability: Emotionally intelligent leaders are skilled at regulating their emotions, especially in high-pressure situations. By staying calm and composed, leaders can maintain a stable and supportive environment for their teams. Self-regulation also involves delaying impulses, meaning that emotionally intelligent leaders don't react impulsively to stress or conflict but take a thoughtful approach to problem-solving.

- Tip: Practice pausing before reacting to challenging situations. Taking a moment to assess your emotional state and considering the best course of action can prevent reactive behaviors that might harm team morale.

Motivation and Inspiring Teams: EI-driven leaders are motivated by more than just external rewards—they are passionate about their work and their vision. This intrinsic motivation is contagious, inspiring teams to align with the leader's enthusiasm and commitment. Leaders who are emotionally intelligent can connect the team's work to a greater purpose, making each team member feel like they're contributing to something meaningful.

- Tip: Regularly communicate the "why" behind your company's goals. Help your team understand how their work fits into the bigger picture and how their contributions are vital to the company's success.

Social Skills and Conflict Resolution: High emotional intelligence improves a leader's social skills, particularly when it comes to managing relationships and resolving conflicts. Leaders with strong EI can navigate interpersonal challenges within the team, diffuse tensions, and turn disagreements into opportunities for learning and growth.

- Tip: When conflicts arise, practice active listening. Allow team members to express their concerns without interruption, and validate their feelings before offering solutions. This approach builds trust and leads to more constructive resolutions.

Practical Ways to Lead with Empathy
Leading with empathy involves more than just understanding how people feel—it requires taking action to support your team and create a positive work environment. Here are some practical ways to lead with empathy:

Active Listening: Active listening is a key skill for empathetic leaders. It involves giving full attention to the person speaking, acknowledging their emotions, and responding thoughtfully. Active listening goes beyond just hearing words—it's about understanding the underlying emotions and motivations behind them.
- Tip: During one-on-one meetings or team discussions, focus fully on the speaker. Avoid distractions like checking emails or thinking about your response while they're talking. After they've finished, reflect back what you've heard to ensure understanding.

Show Genuine Interest in Your Team's Well-Being: Empathetic leaders take the time to check in with their teams, not just about work but also about their personal well-being. This doesn't mean prying into private matters but rather showing concern for their overall health and happiness. Simple gestures, like asking how someone is feeling or offering flexibility when someone is dealing with personal challenges, go a long way in building trust.
- Tip: Make it a habit to ask your team how they're doing at the start of meetings or in casual conversations. Listen attentively to their responses and offer support where needed, whether it's emotional or practical.

Empower Your Team: Empathy isn't about doing everything for your team—it's about understanding their strengths and challenges and empowering them to succeed. Leaders who show empathy delegate responsibility and trust their team members to make decisions, offering guidance and support when needed.
- Tip: Provide opportunities for your team members to take ownership of projects. Empower them to make decisions and offer feedback, but avoid micromanaging. Trusting your team fosters confidence and professional growth.

Recognize and Validate Emotions: Empathetic leaders don't dismiss or minimize the emotions of their team members. Whether someone is feeling stressed, excited, frustrated, or anxious, acknowledging and validating those emotions helps create an environment of psychological safety.
- Tip: If a team member expresses frustration, instead of brushing it aside, respond with validation. For example, you could say, "I can see that this situation is really frustrating for you. Let's talk about how we can address it together."

Promote Work-Life Balance: Empathy also means understanding that your team members have lives outside of work. Leaders who recognize the importance of work-life balance create a healthier, more sustainable work environment. Offering flexibility and encouraging breaks can help prevent burnout and improve overall productivity.
- Tip: Encourage your team to take time off when needed and model work-life balance yourself. When leaders set boundaries around work hours and prioritize their well-being, it sets a positive example for the rest of the team.

Case Study: Empathy in Leadership

Let's look at an example of a leader who used empathy to transform their organization's culture.

Satya Nadella and Microsoft's Transformation

When Satya Nadella became CEO of Microsoft in 2014, the company was facing stagnation and an internal culture of intense competition. Nadella's approach to leadership centered around empathy, and he worked to shift Microsoft's culture towards collaboration, openness, and learning. One of his key initiatives was encouraging a "growth mindset" within the company, where employees were encouraged to learn from mistakes and support each other's development. This culture of empathy and emotional intelligence led to renewed innovation and increased employee satisfaction, helping Microsoft regain its position as a market leader.

Nadella's leadership style highlights the power of empathy in fostering a positive work environment and driving organizational success. By prioritizing people and relationships, Nadella was able to transform Microsoft's internal dynamics, leading to a more resilient and productive company.

The Role of Empathy in Remote Teams
In today's increasingly remote work environment, leading with empathy has become more important than ever. Remote teams face unique challenges, such as feelings of isolation, communication barriers, and difficulty maintaining work-life balance. Empathetic leaders who are attuned to these challenges can provide the support and flexibility their teams need to thrive.

1. Stay Connected: Regular check-ins are crucial for remote teams. Empathetic leaders make an effort to stay connected with their team members, even if it's just a quick message to ask how things are going.
2. Be Flexible: Remote work requires a different level of flexibility. Empathetic leaders understand that team members may need to adjust their schedules to accommodate personal responsibilities and should provide that flexibility whenever possible.
3. Create Opportunities for Social Interaction: Remote work can be isolating, so empathetic leaders create opportunities for team members to connect on a personal level. Virtual coffee breaks, team-building activities, and casual conversations help maintain a sense of community.

Conclusion: The Empathetic Leader's Edge
Leading with empathy and emotional intelligence is not only good for team morale, but it also has a direct impact on business success. Empathetic leaders build trust, foster collaboration, and create an environment where employees feel valued and supported. In today's complex and fast-paced business landscape, leaders who prioritize empathy will be better equipped to navigate challenges, inspire their teams, and drive long-term success.

By embracing empathy as a key leadership tool, entrepreneurs can cultivate high-performing teams that are resilient, engaged, and motivated to achieve shared goals. Emotional intelligence in leadership isn't just about understanding others—it's about using that understanding to create a workplace where everyone can thrive.

Chapter 7: Emotional Intelligence in Decision-Making: How to Make Smarter, More Informed Choices

Good decision-making is a critical skill for entrepreneurs. Whether it's about product development, marketing strategies, or hiring new team members, the quality of decisions can determine the success or failure of a business. However, decision-making isn't just a rational process of analyzing data and weighing pros and cons—it's also deeply influenced by emotions.

This is where emotional intelligence (EI) comes into play. Leaders who are emotionally intelligent are better equipped to recognize and manage the emotional aspects of decision-making. By understanding how emotions can both positively and negatively influence decisions, entrepreneurs can make smarter, more balanced, and effective choices.

The Role of Emotions in Decision-Making

Traditionally, decision-making has been viewed as a purely logical process. However, research in psychology and neuroscience has shown that emotions are deeply intertwined with our decision-making. In fact, emotions often drive our choices more than we realize. Emotional intelligence allows us to recognize when emotions are influencing our decisions, and to either harness those emotions productively or set them aside when necessary.

Emotions Can Cloud Judgment: In some cases, emotions like fear, frustration, or excitement can cloud our judgment, leading to poor decisions. For example, an entrepreneur who is overly optimistic about a new product may ignore potential risks, or a leader under stress might make hasty decisions without considering all the facts.
- Tip: Before making a major decision, take a step back and assess your emotional state. Are you feeling stressed, anxious, or overly excited? Recognizing your emotional state can help you determine whether your emotions are clouding your judgment.

Emotions Can Enhance Creativity and Innovation: On the flip side, emotions can also play a positive role in decision-making, particularly when it comes to creativity and innovation. Emotions like passion, curiosity, and excitement can inspire bold, innovative choices that lead to breakthroughs. Emotionally intelligent leaders know how to tap into these positive emotions without letting them overshadow rational thinking.

- Tip: When making creative decisions, allow yourself to embrace positive emotions like excitement and curiosity, but also balance them with logical analysis to ensure your decision is grounded in reality.

Intuition and Emotional Intelligence: Emotional intelligence is closely linked to intuition, which is often described as the "gut feeling" we experience when making decisions. While intuition can be a valuable tool, it's important to distinguish between intuition driven by deep experience and intuition clouded by biases or strong emotions. Emotionally intelligent leaders are skilled at recognizing when to trust their intuition and when to rely more heavily on logic and data.

- Tip: When faced with a decision, check whether your intuitive response is based on experience and insight or if it's being influenced by emotions like fear or overconfidence.

Key Elements of Emotional Intelligence in Decision-Making
Self-Awareness: Recognizing Emotional Biases
Self-awareness is the foundation of emotional intelligence in decision-making. Leaders who are self-aware can recognize when their emotions are influencing their decisions, either positively or negatively. For example, a self-aware entrepreneur may realize that their fear of failure is leading them to avoid taking necessary risks, or that their excitement over a new idea is causing them to overlook potential challenges.

- Tip: Practice regularly checking in with your emotions before making important decisions. Ask yourself: "What am I feeling right now, and how might it be influencing my choices?"

Self-Regulation: Managing Emotions Under Pressure

Decision-making often happens under pressure, especially in the fast-paced world of entrepreneurship. In these moments, leaders who can regulate their emotions are better able to think clearly and make sound decisions. Self-regulation involves staying calm, composed, and focused, even in stressful situations.

- Tip: Develop strategies for managing stress and pressure, such as taking deep breaths, stepping away from the situation briefly, or practicing mindfulness. These techniques can help you maintain emotional balance during critical decision-making moments.

Empathy: Understanding the Emotions of Others

Empathy is not only important for building relationships with team members—it also plays a crucial role in decision-making. Empathetic leaders are able to consider the emotions and perspectives of others when making decisions, which leads to more inclusive and well-rounded choices. For example, when deciding on a company-wide policy change, an empathetic leader will take into account how that change will impact employees on an emotional level, ensuring that the decision benefits everyone.

- Tip: When making decisions that affect others, actively seek input from your team and consider their emotional responses. This can help you make more informed and empathetic choices.

Motivation: Staying Focused on Long-Term Goals

Emotionally intelligent leaders are able to stay motivated by their long-term goals, even when faced with short-term setbacks or emotional distractions. This motivation helps them make decisions that align with their vision for the future, rather than being swayed by immediate emotions or challenges.

- Tip: Keep your long-term goals in mind when making decisions, and ask yourself whether your choice will move you closer to achieving those goals. This can help you stay focused and avoid making impulsive, emotion-driven decisions.

Practical Strategies for Emotionally Intelligent Decision-Making

Pause and Reflect: One of the simplest and most effective strategies for emotionally intelligent decision-making is to pause and reflect before making a choice. This brief pause gives you the opportunity to assess your emotions and gather your thoughts, preventing impulsive decisions driven by strong emotions.

- Tip: Before making a major decision, take a few moments to pause and reflect. Ask yourself: "What emotions am I feeling right now? Are they helping or hindering my decision-making?"

Seek Diverse Perspectives

Emotionally intelligent leaders recognize that their own emotions and experiences may create blind spots. To make more informed decisions, they seek out diverse perspectives from their team or trusted advisors. This helps them gain a broader understanding of the situation and consider emotions and factors they might have overlooked.

- Tip: When facing a difficult decision, ask for input from people with different perspectives and backgrounds. This can help you see the situation from multiple angles and make a more well-rounded decision.

Practice Mindfulness

Mindfulness is a powerful tool for enhancing emotional intelligence and improving decision-making. By practicing mindfulness, leaders can become more aware of their emotions and thought processes, which helps them stay grounded and focused during decision-making.

- Tip: Incorporate mindfulness practices, such as meditation or deep breathing exercises, into your daily routine. These practices can help you stay calm and centered, even in high-pressure situations.

Balance Emotions and Logic

While emotions play a significant role in decision-making, they should be balanced with logic and data. Emotionally intelligent leaders are able to consider both emotional and rational factors when making decisions, leading to choices that are both empathetic and practical.

- Tip: When making a decision, write down both the emotional and logical factors influencing your choice. This can help you see the full picture and ensure that you're considering both your emotions and the facts.

Case Study: Emotionally Intelligent Decision-Making in Action
Jeff Bezos and Data-Driven Decision-Making at Amazon
Amazon's founder, Jeff Bezos, is known for his data-driven approach to decision-making, but emotional intelligence also plays a key role in his leadership. Bezos has often emphasized the importance of intuition and empathy in decision-making, particularly when it comes to understanding customer needs.

For example, when Amazon was deciding to launch Amazon Prime, the decision wasn't just based on financial data—it was also influenced by a deep understanding of customer emotions. Bezos recognized that customers valued convenience and wanted faster shipping, even if it meant paying a membership fee. This empathetic understanding of customer emotions, combined with data analysis, led to the creation of one of Amazon's most successful services.

Bezos' ability to balance logic with empathy and intuition has been a critical factor in Amazon's success, demonstrating how emotional intelligence can lead to smarter, more customer-focused decisions.

Emotional Intelligence in High-Stakes Decisions
When it comes to high-stakes decisions, such as securing investment, launching a new product, or pivoting a business strategy, emotional intelligence becomes even more crucial. High-stakes decisions often involve significant pressure, uncertainty, and risk, all of which can trigger strong emotions. Emotionally intelligent leaders are able to manage these emotions effectively, ensuring that they don't make rash decisions based on fear or excitement.

Managing Fear in Risky Decisions: Fear of failure is a common emotion in high-stakes decisions. Emotionally intelligent leaders are able to recognize this fear, assess its validity, and make decisions that balance caution with boldness.
- Tip: When making risky decisions, acknowledge your fear but don't let it paralyze you. Consider the risks objectively and develop contingency plans to mitigate potential downsides.

Harnessing Excitement for Innovation: High-stakes decisions often come with excitement, especially when pursuing new opportunities. Emotionally intelligent leaders can harness this excitement to fuel innovation, while also ensuring that their enthusiasm doesn't lead to overly risky choices.
- Tip: Use excitement to drive creativity, but balance it with a careful assessment of potential risks and challenges.

Conclusion: Smarter Decision-Making Through Emotional Intelligence

Emotional intelligence is a powerful tool for improving decision-making. By recognizing and managing emotions—both their own and those of others—entrepreneurs can make more balanced, informed, and effective decisions. Whether it's managing risk, fostering creativity, or navigating high-stakes situations, emotional intelligence helps leaders stay grounded and focused, ensuring that their choices align with both their long-term goals and the needs of their team and customers.

Chapter 8: Conflict Resolution with Emotional Intelligence

Conflict is an inevitable part of any workplace, especially in fast-paced and high-pressure entrepreneurial environments. Disagreements can arise over project directions, resource allocation, or even interpersonal relationships. However, how conflicts are handled can either strengthen a team or drive it apart.

Emotionally intelligent leaders have the skills to approach conflicts in a way that resolves issues effectively while maintaining positive relationships. They can manage their own emotions during tense situations, empathize with others, and use communication strategies to turn conflicts into opportunities for growth and improvement.

Understanding the Emotional Triggers Behind Conflict
At its core, conflict often stems from unmet emotional needs, such as feeling undervalued, misunderstood, or disrespected. Emotionally intelligent leaders are able to identify these emotional triggers and address the underlying causes of the conflict, rather than just the surface-level disagreement. Understanding these emotional drivers allows leaders to respond in a way that defuses tension and fosters understanding.

Emotions in Conflict Escalation: Conflicts often escalate because emotions like frustration, anger, or defensiveness take over. When emotions run high, people become less rational and more reactive, which can turn a small disagreement into a full-blown argument. Emotional intelligence helps leaders recognize when emotions are escalating and step in to manage the situation before it spirals out of control.
- Tip: When you sense a conflict is escalating, pause and take a moment to assess the emotional dynamics at play. Address the emotions first by acknowledging how people are feeling, which can help defuse the situation.

The Role of Empathy in Conflict Resolution: Empathy is a key component of emotional intelligence and one of the most powerful tools for resolving conflict. When leaders demonstrate empathy, they show that they are genuinely trying to understand the other person's perspective and emotions. This can build trust and open the door to constructive dialogue.

- Tip: Practice active listening during conflicts. Instead of focusing on how to defend your position, focus on truly understanding the other person's concerns and emotions.

Self-Regulation: Staying Calm Under Pressure: During conflicts, it's easy to get emotionally charged, especially if you feel attacked or frustrated. Emotionally intelligent leaders are able to regulate their emotions, staying calm and composed even in heated situations. This calm demeanor helps prevent the conflict from escalating and sets the tone for a more productive conversation.

- Tip: If you feel your emotions rising during a conflict, take a deep breath or step away from the situation briefly. This will give you the space to regain your composure and approach the conflict with a level head.

Strategies for Emotionally Intelligent Conflict Resolution
Seek to Understand, Then Be Understood: One of the most effective ways to resolve conflicts is to first seek to understand the other person's point of view before trying to explain your own. This approach not only helps to uncover the root cause of the conflict, but it also shows that you value the other person's perspective. When people feel heard, they are more likely to be open to finding a solution.

- Tip: Start conflict resolution conversations by asking questions like, "Can you help me understand your concerns?" or "What's most important to you in this situation?"

Focus on Interests, Not Positions: In many conflicts, people become entrenched in their positions ("I want this to happen!") without realizing that their positions are often driven by underlying interests or needs.

Emotionally intelligent leaders know how to shift the conversation from fixed positions to deeper interests. This creates the possibility for win-win solutions that meet everyone's needs.
- Tip: Instead of debating positions, ask questions like, "Why is this important to you?" or "What are you hoping to achieve with this solution?" This helps uncover the real issues at stake.

Use "I" Statements to Communicate Feelings: During conflicts, it's common for people to express their frustrations in ways that can come across as accusatory or blameful. For example, saying "You never listen to me!" can put the other person on the defensive. Emotionally intelligent leaders use "I" statements to express how they feel without placing blame, which can help reduce defensiveness and open the door to more productive communication.
- Tip: Instead of saying, "You're not listening," try saying, "I feel unheard when I try to share my thoughts." This shifts the focus to your feelings and reduces the likelihood of the other person feeling attacked.

Find Common Ground: Emotionally intelligent leaders are skilled at finding common ground, even in the midst of conflict. By identifying shared goals or values, they can help bring people together and shift the conversation from conflict to collaboration. This approach encourages a solution-focused mindset and reduces the tension between opposing sides.
- Tip: Look for areas of agreement or shared interests. For example, you might say, "We both want the project to succeed, so let's figure out how we can achieve that together."

Managing Team Dynamics During Conflict
When conflict arises within a team, it's important for leaders to address it quickly and effectively to prevent it from damaging morale or productivity. Emotionally intelligent leaders understand that unresolved conflicts can fester and create a toxic work environment, so they take proactive steps to manage team dynamics during disagreements.

Encourage Open Dialogue: Emotionally intelligent leaders create an environment where team members feel safe to express their concerns and disagreements openly. This prevents conflicts from simmering under the surface and gives leaders the opportunity to address issues before they escalate.
- Tip: Hold regular team meetings where team members are encouraged to voice their concerns in a constructive manner. Create ground rules for respectful communication and make sure everyone has a chance to speak.

Mediate When Necessary: In some cases, leaders may need to step in as mediators when conflicts arise between team members. The goal of mediation is to facilitate a conversation where both parties feel heard and understood, and to help them find a solution that works for everyone. Emotionally intelligent leaders remain neutral during mediation and focus on guiding the conversation toward a positive resolution.
- Tip: When mediating a conflict, avoid taking sides. Instead, ask each party to share their perspective, listen actively, and help them find areas of agreement or compromise.

Promote a Culture of Respect and Empathy: Emotionally intelligent leaders foster a culture of respect and empathy within their teams. By modeling empathetic behavior and encouraging respectful communication, they create an environment where conflicts are less likely to escalate and more likely to be resolved constructively.
- Tip: Lead by example by treating everyone with respect, even during disagreements. Encourage team members to do the same and hold them accountable for maintaining a respectful tone in all communications.

Case Study: Conflict Resolution with Emotional Intelligence
Howard Schultz and Starbucks' Inclusive Leadership
Howard Schultz, the former CEO of Starbucks, is known for his empathetic leadership style and his approach to resolving conflicts within the company.

When Starbucks faced internal conflicts over pay disparities and workplace conditions, Schultz used emotional intelligence to address the concerns of employees and stakeholders.

Schultz recognized that the root of the conflict wasn't just about wages—it was about employees feeling undervalued and unheard. Instead of dismissing their concerns, Schultz initiated open conversations with employees, listened to their grievances, and implemented changes that reflected their needs. His emotionally intelligent approach to conflict resolution not only improved employee morale but also strengthened Starbucks' reputation as an inclusive and compassionate employer.

This case illustrates how emotionally intelligent conflict resolution can lead to positive outcomes for both the business and its employees.

Preventing Conflicts Through Emotional Intelligence
While it's important to know how to resolve conflicts, emotionally intelligent leaders also take steps to prevent conflicts from arising in the first place. By fostering an environment of open communication, mutual respect, and emotional awareness, they can reduce the likelihood of misunderstandings and disagreements.

Encourage Emotional Expression: Leaders who encourage emotional expression create a workplace where team members feel comfortable sharing their feelings and concerns before they escalate into conflicts. This proactive approach allows leaders to address issues early on, preventing them from turning into larger problems.
- Tip: Create channels for open communication, such as regular check-ins or anonymous feedback systems, where team members can express their concerns without fear of judgment.

Build Strong Relationships with Team Members: Leaders who invest in building strong, trust-based relationships with their team members are better able to prevent conflicts. When team members feel valued, respected, and understood, they are less likely to engage in unnecessary disputes.

- Tip: Make time to build personal connections with your team. Show genuine interest in their well-being and foster a sense of belonging and support within the team.

Conclusion: Transforming Conflict into Collaboration

Emotionally intelligent leaders view conflict not as a roadblock, but as an opportunity for growth, learning, and collaboration. By recognizing the emotional dynamics at play, practicing empathy, and fostering open communication, leaders can resolve conflicts in a way that strengthens relationships and enhances team performance. Conflict, when handled with emotional intelligence, becomes a catalyst for innovation, creativity, and stronger bonds within the team.

Chapter 9: Building Resilience Through Emotional Intelligence

Resilience is the ability to bounce back from adversity, adapt to change, and keep moving forward despite challenges. In the fast-paced and unpredictable world of entrepreneurship, resilience is an essential quality for long-term success. But resilience isn't just about "toughing it out"—it requires emotional intelligence to navigate difficult situations with clarity, maintain emotional balance, and cultivate the inner strength needed to persevere.

In this chapter, we'll explore how emotional intelligence can be a powerful tool for building resilience, both for entrepreneurs and their teams. By mastering self-awareness, emotional regulation, and empathy, emotionally intelligent leaders can foster a culture of resilience that helps their businesses thrive, even in the face of setbacks.

The Role of Emotional Intelligence in Building Resilience
At its core, emotional intelligence helps leaders understand and manage their emotions, stay calm under pressure, and maintain perspective during difficult times. These qualities are essential for building resilience, as they allow entrepreneurs to stay grounded and focused, even in the most challenging circumstances.

Self-Awareness: Understanding Your Emotional Triggers
Self-awareness is the foundation of emotional intelligence and plays a key role in resilience. Emotionally intelligent leaders are aware of their emotional triggers and know how to manage them effectively. This self-awareness helps them recognize when they are feeling overwhelmed, anxious, or stressed, allowing them to take proactive steps to address these emotions before they escalate.
- Tip: Regularly check in with yourself to assess your emotional state, especially during times of stress. Acknowledge your emotions without judgment and take time to reflect on how they may be influencing your thoughts and decisions.

Self-Regulation: Managing Stress and Maintaining Composure
Resilience isn't about avoiding stress—it's about managing it in a way that allows you to stay composed and focused on your goals. Emotionally intelligent leaders use self-regulation techniques to keep their emotions in check during difficult times. By staying calm and composed, they can think more clearly and make better decisions, even in high-pressure situations.
- Tip: When faced with a stressful situation, practice deep breathing or mindfulness techniques to calm your mind and body. This will help you regulate your emotions and approach the situation with a clear and focused mindset.

Empathy: Building Strong Support Systems: Resilient leaders understand the importance of support systems, both in their personal lives and within their teams. Emotional intelligence helps leaders build strong, trusting relationships with others, creating a network of support that they can rely on during tough times. Empathy plays a crucial role in this, as it allows leaders to connect with others on a deeper level and foster a sense of community and mutual support.
- Tip: Cultivate empathy within your team by creating a culture of openness and understanding. Encourage team members to support one another during difficult times and show genuine concern for their well-being.

Optimism: Reframing Challenges as Opportunities
Emotionally intelligent leaders are able to maintain a positive outlook, even in the face of setbacks. This doesn't mean ignoring challenges—it means reframing them as opportunities for growth and learning. Optimism helps leaders stay resilient by keeping them focused on the long-term vision, rather than getting bogged down by temporary obstacles.
- Tip: When faced with a setback, practice cognitive reappraisal by asking yourself, "What can I learn from this experience?" or "How can I use this challenge to become stronger?" This shift in perspective can help you stay motivated and resilient.

Resilience in Action: Leading Through Adversity

Building resilience as an entrepreneur involves not only developing your own emotional intelligence but also fostering resilience within your team. Emotionally intelligent leaders create an environment where team members feel supported, valued, and empowered to navigate challenges with confidence.

Fostering a Culture of Psychological Safety

Psychological safety is the belief that you can take risks, voice your opinions, and make mistakes without fear of punishment or humiliation. Emotionally intelligent leaders foster a culture of psychological safety within their teams, creating an environment where employees feel comfortable speaking up and taking risks without fear of negative consequences. This sense of safety allows teams to navigate challenges more effectively and recover from setbacks with greater resilience.

- Tip: Encourage open communication within your team and make it clear that mistakes are opportunities for learning, not for blame. Lead by example by being transparent about your own challenges and failures, and how you overcame them.

Encouraging a Growth Mindset

Resilience is closely linked to a growth mindset—the belief that abilities and intelligence can be developed through hard work, learning, and perseverance. Emotionally intelligent leaders promote a growth mindset within their teams, encouraging employees to see challenges as opportunities to improve and grow, rather than as insurmountable obstacles.

- Tip: When team members face setbacks, encourage them to reflect on what they can learn from the experience. Provide feedback and support that helps them see how they can use the challenge to grow and develop new skills.

Leading with Compassion During Tough Times
During periods of adversity, emotionally intelligent leaders lead with compassion. They understand that their team members may be feeling stressed, anxious, or overwhelmed, and they respond with empathy and support. Compassionate leadership fosters trust and loyalty, helping teams stay resilient and united, even in the face of difficult circumstances.
- Tip: Check in with your team regularly, especially during challenging times. Offer emotional support, listen to their concerns, and provide resources or flexibility to help them manage stress.

Building Team Resilience Through Shared Purpose
One of the most powerful ways to build resilience in a team is to create a strong sense of shared purpose. Emotionally intelligent leaders inspire their teams by connecting their work to a greater mission or vision. When team members feel that they are working toward a meaningful goal, they are more likely to stay motivated and resilient, even when facing challenges.
- Tip: Regularly communicate the "why" behind your team's work. Remind them of the bigger picture and how their efforts contribute to the overall success of the business. This sense of purpose can help them stay focused and resilient in the face of adversity.

Building Personal Resilience as an Entrepreneur
Entrepreneurship is full of ups and downs, and building personal resilience is key to staying strong and adaptable throughout your journey. Emotionally intelligent leaders use a combination of self-care, emotional awareness, and positive thinking to maintain their resilience.

Prioritizing Self-Care
Resilience is not just a mental skill—it's also closely tied to physical well-being. Emotionally intelligent leaders recognize the importance of self-care and prioritize their physical and mental health. This includes getting enough sleep, exercising regularly, and taking time to relax and recharge.
- Tip: Make self-care a non-negotiable part of your routine. Schedule regular breaks, set boundaries around work hours, and prioritize activities that help you relax and de-stress.

Practicing Mindfulness and Emotional Awareness
Mindfulness is a powerful tool for building resilience, as it helps leaders stay present and aware of their emotions. By practicing mindfulness, entrepreneurs can improve their ability to manage stress, stay calm under pressure, and maintain emotional balance.
- Tip: Incorporate mindfulness practices, such as meditation or deep breathing, into your daily routine. This can help you stay grounded and focused, even during challenging times.

Embracing Failure as a Learning Opportunity
Failure is a natural part of entrepreneurship, but resilient leaders don't let it define them. Instead, they use failure as an opportunity to learn, grow, and improve. Emotionally intelligent leaders are able to reframe failure as a stepping stone to success, allowing them to bounce back from setbacks with a positive attitude.
- Tip: When you experience a failure or setback, take time to reflect on what went wrong and what you can learn from the experience. This mindset shift can help you view challenges as opportunities for growth, rather than as personal defeats.

Surrounding Yourself with Supportive Relationships
Resilience is often strengthened by the relationships we build. Emotionally intelligent leaders surround themselves with supportive mentors, peers, and loved ones who provide encouragement, advice, and perspective during difficult times.
- Tip: Build a network of supportive people who understand the challenges of entrepreneurship. Regularly reach out to your support system for guidance, encouragement, and emotional support.

Case Study: Building Resilience Through Emotional Intelligence
Oprah Winfrey's Journey of Resilience
Oprah Winfrey's life and career are a testament to the power of resilience and emotional intelligence. From overcoming a difficult childhood marked by poverty and abuse to becoming one of the most successful media moguls in the world, Winfrey's journey is filled with challenges and setbacks.

However, her ability to stay resilient in the face of adversity has been key to her success.

Throughout her career, Winfrey has demonstrated a high level of emotional intelligence, particularly in her ability to understand and manage her emotions, connect deeply with others, and stay focused on her long-term vision. She has often spoken about the importance of self-awareness, mindfulness, and surrounding herself with a supportive network of friends and mentors who have helped her navigate the ups and downs of her career.

Winfrey's story illustrates how emotional intelligence can help entrepreneurs build resilience and thrive, even when faced with significant challenges.

Conclusion: Building Long-Term Resilience Through Emotional Intelligence
Resilience is not about avoiding challenges—it's about developing the emotional intelligence needed to navigate them with grace, determination, and a positive mindset. Emotionally intelligent leaders are able to build resilience by staying self-aware, managing their emotions effectively, and fostering strong support systems within their teams. By creating a culture of resilience, entrepreneurs can ensure that both they and their teams are prepared to handle whatever challenges come their way.

Resilience, like emotional intelligence, is a skill that can be developed over time. With the right tools and mindset, emotionally intelligent leaders can build the inner strength needed to persevere through adversity, achieve their goals, and lead their teams to long-term success.

Chapter 10: Emotional Agility: Adapting Quickly to Change and Uncertainty

In the modern business landscape, change and uncertainty are inevitable. Markets shift, technologies evolve, and unexpected disruptions can arise at any moment. For entrepreneurs, the ability to remain flexible and adapt quickly to these changes is essential for long-term success. This ability is known as emotional agility—the capacity to manage emotions effectively, stay open to new possibilities, and make quick, thoughtful adjustments in response to changing circumstances.

Emotional agility is a crucial component of emotional intelligence. It enables leaders to navigate uncertainty with confidence, embrace change as an opportunity, and maintain their emotional balance in the face of challenges. In this chapter, we'll explore how emotionally intelligent leaders develop emotional agility and use it to lead their businesses through periods of rapid change and unpredictability.

What is Emotional Agility?
Emotional agility, a term popularized by psychologist Dr. Susan David, refers to the ability to manage one's thoughts and emotions in a way that aligns with core values, even in the face of difficult situations. It involves being emotionally flexible, accepting emotions without becoming overwhelmed by them, and making decisions that reflect both short-term needs and long-term goals.

For entrepreneurs, emotional agility is essential for adapting to the fast pace of change in business. Emotionally agile leaders are able to:
- Recognize and accept their emotions, even when they are uncomfortable.
- Pause and reflect before reacting to challenging situations.
- Stay curious, open to new ideas, and willing to pivot when necessary.
- Make quick, confident decisions while maintaining emotional balance.

The Importance of Emotional Agility in Business

Entrepreneurship is full of uncertainties, from market volatility to customer behavior shifts and unexpected crises like economic downturns or global pandemics. Leaders who are emotionally agile can remain calm and composed during times of uncertainty, helping them make better decisions and lead their teams with confidence.

Navigating Change with Emotional Flexibility

Emotionally agile leaders are able to adapt to new circumstances without being derailed by fear, frustration, or resistance. They understand that change is a constant in business, and instead of clinging to old ways of doing things, they are open to exploring new strategies, technologies, or processes.

- Tip: When faced with a change, take a moment to acknowledge any discomfort or resistance you might be feeling. Recognize that these emotions are natural, but don't let them dictate your actions. Focus on staying open to new possibilities and approaches.

Managing Uncertainty with Composure

Uncertainty can trigger anxiety and fear, which can cloud judgment and lead to poor decision-making. Emotionally agile leaders manage these emotions by acknowledging their uncertainty, reframing it as a natural part of business, and focusing on what they can control. This helps them stay calm and composed, even in the face of unpredictable challenges.

- Tip: When uncertainty arises, shift your focus to what you can control. Identify specific actions you can take to address the situation, and let go of the things that are beyond your control.

Embracing a Growth Mindset in Times of Change

Emotionally agile leaders embrace change with a growth mindset—the belief that challenges are opportunities for learning and development. Instead of seeing change as a threat, they view it as an opportunity to innovate, improve, and grow. This mindset not only helps leaders adapt quickly to change but also inspires their teams to do the same.

- Tip: When faced with a challenge or change, ask yourself, "What can I learn from this?" or "How can this situation help me or my team grow?" This shift in perspective will help you stay resilient and proactive in the face of change.

Emotional Intelligence Skills for Developing Emotional Agility
Developing emotional agility requires a combination of emotional intelligence skills, including self-awareness, self-regulation, empathy, and cognitive flexibility. Let's explore how these EI skills contribute to emotional agility and how you can cultivate them as an entrepreneur.

Self-Awareness: Recognizing Emotional Responses to Change
The first step in developing emotional agility is recognizing your emotional responses to change and uncertainty. Emotionally intelligent leaders are self-aware—they understand how their emotions are influencing their thoughts and behaviors, and they can identify when they are feeling anxious, stressed, or resistant to change.
- Tip: Practice mindfulness to enhance your self-awareness. Regularly check in with yourself to notice your emotional state, especially during times of change. Acknowledge your emotions without judgment and reflect on how they are influencing your decision-making.

Self-Regulation: Staying Emotionally Balanced in Uncertain Times
Self-regulation is the ability to manage your emotions and impulses in a healthy and constructive way. Emotionally agile leaders are skilled at regulating their emotions during times of uncertainty, allowing them to remain calm, composed, and focused on finding solutions.
- Tip: Use techniques like deep breathing, meditation, or short breaks to calm your mind and body when emotions are running high. This will help you stay centered and focused, even in the face of uncertainty.

Empathy: Understanding How Change Affects Others
Emotionally agile leaders don't just focus on their own emotional responses—they also consider how change and uncertainty are affecting their team members. Empathy allows leaders to recognize the emotions of others, understand their concerns, and provide support and guidance during times of change.
- Tip: When leading your team through change, take time to listen to their concerns and validate their emotions. Show empathy by offering support, answering questions, and helping them navigate the uncertainty with confidence.

Cognitive Flexibility: Adapting Your Thinking to New Situations
Cognitive flexibility is the ability to shift your thinking and adapt to new situations. Emotionally agile leaders are open to new ideas, perspectives, and approaches. They are willing to pivot their strategies when necessary and are not rigidly attached to old ways of doing things.
- Tip: When faced with a new challenge or opportunity, practice thinking outside the box. Consider alternative solutions, ask for input from others, and stay open to different ways of approaching the situation.

Practical Strategies for Developing Emotional Agility
Emotional agility is a skill that can be developed with practice. Here are some practical strategies for cultivating emotional agility in your leadership:

Practice Acceptance and Non-Judgment: One of the key aspects of emotional agility is accepting your emotions without judgment. Emotionally agile leaders don't suppress or deny their emotions—they acknowledge them, understand them, and use them as valuable information to guide their decisions.
- Tip: When you notice uncomfortable emotions like fear, frustration, or anxiety, practice accepting them without judgment. Remind yourself that it's okay to feel these emotions, and instead of resisting them, use them as a signal to pause, reflect, and make thoughtful decisions.

Stay Curious and Open-Minded: Emotional agility involves staying curious and open-minded in the face of change. Instead of clinging to old solutions or approaches, emotionally agile leaders are willing to experiment, explore new possibilities, and adapt to changing circumstances.
- Tip: Adopt a mindset of curiosity during times of change. Ask yourself, "What new opportunities might this change present?" or "How can I approach this situation in a fresh, innovative way?"

Cultivate a Problem-Solving Mindset: Emotionally agile leaders focus on finding solutions rather than dwelling on problems. When faced with challenges, they shift their focus to action and problem-solving, rather than getting stuck in frustration or fear.
- Tip: When challenges arise, focus on actionable steps you can take to address the issue. Break down the problem into smaller, manageable tasks, and tackle them one at a time. This proactive approach will help you stay focused and resilient.

Build a Resilient Support System: Emotional agility is strengthened by having a supportive network of peers, mentors, and team members. Emotionally agile leaders surround themselves with people who offer encouragement, advice, and perspective during times of change.
- Tip: Build strong relationships with people who support your growth and development. Regularly seek out feedback, advice, and guidance from your network to help you navigate change and uncertainty with confidence.

Emotional Agility in Action: Leading Through Uncertainty
Let's look at an example of how emotional agility has helped a leader navigate uncertainty and change.

Reed Hastings and the Evolution of Netflix
Reed Hastings, the co-founder and CEO of Netflix, is a prime example of emotional agility in leadership.

Over the years, Hastings has led Netflix through several major transformations, including the shift from DVD rentals to streaming services, the move into original content production, and the expansion into international markets.

Each of these transitions involved significant uncertainty and risk, but Hastings demonstrated emotional agility by staying open to change, embracing new opportunities, and managing his emotions throughout the process. His ability to adapt quickly and make thoughtful, bold decisions has been a key factor in Netflix's success as a global leader in the entertainment industry.

Hastings' leadership shows that emotional agility—staying flexible, open-minded, and emotionally balanced—can help entrepreneurs navigate even the most disruptive changes in their industries.

Building Emotional Agility Within Your Team
As a leader, one of your most important roles is to help your team develop emotional agility. Teams that are emotionally agile can adapt quickly to change, embrace new challenges, and stay resilient in the face of uncertainty. Here are some ways to foster emotional agility within your team:

Encourage Open Dialogue About Change: Emotionally agile teams are able to discuss changes and challenges openly, without fear of judgment. Encourage your team to express their thoughts, concerns, and emotions about upcoming changes, and create a safe space for them to share their perspectives.
- Tip: Hold regular team meetings where you discuss any changes or uncertainties on the horizon. Ask team members how they feel about the changes and what support they need to navigate them.

Promote a Growth Mindset: Foster a culture of growth and learning within your team by encouraging them to view challenges as opportunities for development.

When team members see change as a chance to learn and grow, they are more likely to embrace it with confidence.
- Tip: When your team faces a challenge, ask them what they can learn from the situation and how they can use it to improve. Celebrate both successes and failures as valuable learning experiences.

Model Emotional Agility: As a leader, your team looks to you for cues on how to handle change and uncertainty. By modeling emotional agility—staying calm, open-minded, and flexible—you can inspire your team to do the same.
- Tip: During times of change, be transparent about your own emotional responses, and show your team how you are working through them in a constructive way. This helps normalize emotional agility and encourages your team to develop the same skills.

Conclusion: Thriving Through Change with Emotional Agility
In today's rapidly changing business environment, emotional agility is an essential skill for entrepreneurs. Emotionally agile leaders are able to manage their emotions effectively, stay open to new possibilities, and adapt quickly to change and uncertainty. By cultivating emotional intelligence skills like self-awareness, empathy, and cognitive flexibility, entrepreneurs can navigate the challenges of entrepreneurship with confidence and resilience.

Emotional agility is not just about surviving change—it's about thriving in it. By embracing change as an opportunity for growth and staying emotionally flexible, entrepreneurs can lead their businesses through uncertainty and emerge stronger on the other side.

Chapter 11: Leading Teams Through Organizational Change

Organizational change is inevitable in the life of any business. Whether it's a restructuring, adopting new technologies, entering new markets, or responding to an economic shift, change often brings uncertainty and disruption. As a leader, how you manage these transitions can significantly impact your team's morale, performance, and resilience. Emotionally intelligent leaders understand that organizational change isn't just about logistical adjustments—it's about managing people's emotions and helping them navigate through uncertainty with confidence and clarity.

In this chapter, we'll explore how emotionally intelligent leadership can make all the difference when leading teams through periods of organizational change. By using empathy, clear communication, and emotional support, leaders can guide their teams to not only survive change but thrive through it.

The Emotional Impact of Change on Teams
Change often triggers a wide range of emotions among team members—anxiety, fear, confusion, or even resistance. For some, change might represent opportunity and growth, while for others, it may evoke uncertainty and stress. Emotionally intelligent leaders recognize that people respond to change differently and that these emotions must be addressed for the team to move forward cohesively.

Recognizing Emotional Responses to Change: The emotional reactions of team members to change are often tied to their need for stability and control. When things feel uncertain, people may become anxious or defensive. Emotional intelligence helps leaders recognize these emotional responses early, enabling them to provide support before emotions escalate and impact performance.
- Tip: Pay attention to the emotional cues of your team members, such as changes in behavior, mood, or engagement levels. Acknowledge these emotions and create a space where team members feel comfortable expressing their concerns.

Empathy: Understanding the Human Side of Change
Empathy is crucial when leading teams through change. By putting yourself in your team members' shoes, you can better understand their fears and concerns, which allows you to address them more effectively. Empathetic leadership helps build trust and creates a sense of psychological safety, where team members feel supported and understood during times of transition.
- Tip: During one-on-one meetings or team discussions, ask open-ended questions like, "How are you feeling about the changes?" or "What concerns do you have about the transition?" Listening empathetically will help you understand your team's emotional landscape and offer the right support.

Emotional Agility: Staying Flexible Through the Unknown
Emotionally intelligent leaders maintain their own emotional agility in the face of organizational change. They recognize that change is fluid, and they must stay adaptable to adjust their strategies as new challenges and opportunities arise. This emotional flexibility helps leaders guide their teams more effectively through the uncertainties of the transition.
- Tip: Stay open to feedback and be willing to pivot your approach as needed. Let your team know that you are flexible and adaptable, which can help ease their anxieties about the unknown.

Key Emotional Intelligence Skills for Leading Through Change
Self-Awareness: Understanding Your Own Emotions During Change
Self-awareness is the foundation of emotional intelligence, and it plays a critical role during organizational change. Leaders must first understand their own emotional responses to change before they can effectively guide others. If you're feeling anxious, overwhelmed, or uncertain about the changes, it's essential to recognize these feelings and manage them so they don't affect your leadership.
- Tip: Take time for self-reflection to assess your emotional state during periods of change. Be honest with yourself about any feelings of stress or uncertainty, and develop strategies to manage these emotions, such as mindfulness practices or seeking support from peers.

Self-Regulation: Managing Your Emotions in High-Pressure Situations
Leaders who can self-regulate their emotions during organizational change create a calming and stabilizing presence for their teams. When a leader remains calm and composed, it reassures the team that the situation is under control, even if there are uncertainties. Self-regulation also helps leaders make clear-headed decisions during high-pressure situations, preventing impulsive reactions that could exacerbate team anxieties.
- Tip: Practice techniques like deep breathing, pausing before responding, and taking breaks when you feel emotionally charged. These techniques can help you stay composed and prevent emotional reactions from influencing your leadership decisions.

Communication: Providing Clarity and Transparency
One of the most important aspects of leading through change is clear and transparent communication. When people are unsure of what's happening, anxiety and rumors can spread quickly. Emotionally intelligent leaders ensure that their team members are well-informed, providing regular updates and explaining the reasons behind the change.
- Tip: Hold regular meetings to communicate updates about the change, even if the information is limited. Be transparent about what you know and what is still uncertain, and always invite questions from your team to address any concerns.

Motivation: Inspiring and Engaging Your Team During Transitions
During times of change, it's easy for team members to feel disengaged or lose sight of the bigger picture. Emotionally intelligent leaders keep their teams motivated by reminding them of the organization's mission, vision, and long-term goals. They help team members understand how the change aligns with the broader objectives and what opportunities it may bring for personal and professional growth.
- Tip: Reconnect your team with the organization's purpose. Use language that emphasizes the positive aspects of the change, such as new opportunities for innovation, growth, or improvement.

Managing Resistance to Change
Resistance to change is natural, especially when people feel uncertain or fearful about the future. Emotionally intelligent leaders recognize that resistance often stems from these emotional responses, and they approach it with empathy and understanding.

Identifying the Root Causes of Resistance: Resistance to change can manifest in different ways—whether it's open opposition, passive disengagement, or subtle pushback. Emotionally intelligent leaders seek to understand the underlying reasons for this resistance, which could range from fear of losing control, concern over job security, or discomfort with new responsibilities.
- Tip: Have individual conversations with team members who are resistant to change to understand their concerns. Ask questions like, "What specifically are you worried about?" or "How can I help you feel more comfortable with the transition?"

Involving Your Team in the Change Process: One of the best ways to manage resistance is to involve your team in the change process. When people feel like they have a say in how the change is implemented, they are more likely to embrace it. Emotionally intelligent leaders empower their teams by seeking their input, giving them a sense of ownership, and including them in decision-making whenever possible.
- Tip: Encourage your team to share their ideas on how the change can be implemented more smoothly. This not only helps you gather valuable insights but also gives your team a greater sense of control and investment in the process.

Providing Emotional Support During Transition: Change can be emotionally challenging for many people, and emotionally intelligent leaders provide the support needed to help their team members navigate these emotions. This might include offering additional resources, such as access to counseling services, or simply being available to listen to concerns and provide reassurance.

- Tip: Be available and approachable for your team members during times of change. Let them know that you are there to support them and that it's okay to feel uncertain or anxious. Offer flexibility when possible, such as adjusting workloads or deadlines to ease the pressure during the transition.

Case Study: Leading Organizational Change with Emotional Intelligence
Indra Nooyi and PepsiCo's Transformation
When Indra Nooyi became CEO of PepsiCo, she faced the challenge of transforming the company's focus from traditional soft drinks and snacks to healthier products in response to changing consumer preferences. This organizational change required significant shifts in strategy, product development, and company culture.

Nooyi led this transformation with emotional intelligence, using empathy, transparency, and effective communication to guide her team through the process. She openly acknowledged the difficulties of the transition, while also emphasizing the importance of adapting to consumer demands and staying ahead of market trends. Nooyi involved her team in the decision-making process and consistently communicated the long-term vision for PepsiCo's growth.

Her emotionally intelligent approach helped PepsiCo navigate the organizational change successfully, creating a more agile and future-focused company. By addressing the emotional impact of change and providing clear guidance, Nooyi maintained team morale and drove positive outcomes for the business.

Building Resilience During Organizational Change
Resilience is a key factor in navigating organizational change successfully. Emotionally intelligent leaders help build resilience within their teams by fostering an environment of support, adaptability, and trust.

Encourage Adaptability and Flexibility: Change often requires new skills, processes, or ways of thinking. Emotionally intelligent leaders encourage their teams to stay adaptable and flexible, helping them develop the skills needed to thrive in the new environment.
- Tip: Provide training and development opportunities to help your team adapt to the changes. Encourage them to view the transition as an opportunity to learn new skills and grow in their roles.

Foster a Sense of Community and Support: During times of change, teams are more likely to stay resilient if they feel supported by their peers and leaders. Emotionally intelligent leaders foster a sense of community within their teams by encouraging collaboration, mutual support, and open communication.
- Tip: Create opportunities for team members to collaborate and support each other during the transition. This could include team-building activities, peer mentoring, or simply encouraging team members to check in with one another regularly.

Celebrate Milestones and Progress: Organizational change can be a long and challenging process, so it's important to recognize and celebrate the progress along the way. Emotionally intelligent leaders celebrate small wins, reinforcing the team's efforts and keeping them motivated.
- Tip: Acknowledge milestones during the change process, no matter how small. Celebrating progress helps maintain morale and reminds the team that their hard work is paying off.

Conclusion: Guiding Teams Through Change with Emotional Intelligence
Leading teams through organizational change requires more than just a strategic plan—it requires emotional intelligence. By recognizing the emotional impact of change, providing empathy and support, and maintaining clear communication, emotionally intelligent leaders can help their teams navigate transitions with confidence and resilience.

Change can be challenging, but it also presents opportunities for growth, innovation, and improvement. Emotionally intelligent leaders not only guide their teams through the difficulties of change but also inspire them to embrace the possibilities it brings. With emotional agility, empathy, and resilience, entrepreneurs can lead their businesses through even the most complex organizational changes, emerging stronger and more adaptable on the other side.

Chapter 12: The Future of Emotional Intelligence in Business: Trends and Predictions

As businesses continue to evolve in response to technological advancements, globalization, and changing workplace dynamics, emotional intelligence (EI) is becoming increasingly recognized as a critical leadership and organizational skill. The ability to navigate complex emotions, build meaningful relationships, and foster collaboration is more valuable than ever, especially as businesses face challenges that are not just technical but human-centered.

In this chapter, we will explore the future of emotional intelligence in business, examining emerging trends and predictions for how EI will continue to shape leadership, team dynamics, and organizational success in the years to come.

The Growing Importance of Emotional Intelligence in Business

As we move further into the 21st century, the demand for emotionally intelligent leaders is only increasing. Several key trends are contributing to this growing importance:

Remote Work and Virtual Teams: The rise of remote work, accelerated by the COVID-19 pandemic, has fundamentally changed the way teams communicate and collaborate. Emotional intelligence plays a crucial role in leading remote teams, as leaders must navigate the challenges of building trust, maintaining engagement, and fostering strong relationships without the benefit of face-to-face interaction.

- Prediction: As remote work continues to be a prominent feature of modern businesses, leaders with high emotional intelligence will be essential for maintaining team cohesion, morale, and productivity in virtual environments.

Diversity, Equity, and Inclusion (DEI): Organizations are increasingly prioritizing diversity, equity, and inclusion as core values. Emotional intelligence is at the heart of creating inclusive workplaces, as it enables leaders to empathize with diverse perspectives, foster belonging, and address bias effectively.

- Prediction: Emotional intelligence will become a central skill for DEI initiatives, as leaders who can navigate complex cultural dynamics and show empathy will be critical in creating workplaces where everyone feels valued and respected.

Artificial Intelligence and Human Skills: As artificial intelligence (AI) and automation take over more routine tasks, the value of human skills—such as emotional intelligence—will become even more pronounced. While AI excels at processing data and performing technical tasks, it lacks the ability to understand and respond to human emotions. This makes emotional intelligence a key differentiator for leaders and employees in an increasingly automated world.
- Prediction: Emotional intelligence will be seen as one of the most important skills in the workplace of the future, complementing technological advancements and providing the human touch that AI cannot replicate.

Mental Health and Well-Being: The focus on mental health and well-being in the workplace is growing, with more organizations recognizing the impact of stress, burnout, and emotional exhaustion on employee performance. Emotionally intelligent leaders are better equipped to create supportive environments where mental health is prioritized, and employees feel safe to express their emotions.
- Prediction: The emphasis on mental health and well-being will increase, and emotionally intelligent leaders will play a key role in creating workplace cultures that prioritize employee well-being, helping to reduce burnout and improve overall productivity.

Trends in Emotional Intelligence Development
With the growing demand for emotional intelligence in business, there are several key trends emerging in the development of EI skills among leaders and employees:

Emotional Intelligence Training and Development Programs: As emotional intelligence becomes a core leadership skill, organizations are investing more in EI training and development programs. These programs are designed to help leaders and employees build self-awareness, empathy, and emotional regulation, all of which contribute to improved performance and collaboration.
- Prediction: Emotional intelligence training will become a standard part of leadership development programs, with organizations investing in workshops, coaching, and online courses to help their teams build EI skills.

AI and EI Integration: Interestingly, AI technology is now being used to enhance emotional intelligence in the workplace. From emotion-tracking tools to AI-powered emotional assessments, technology is helping organizations measure and develop EI in more objective and data-driven ways.
- Prediction: AI-driven tools will increasingly be used to help leaders and employees assess and improve their emotional intelligence. These tools will provide personalized feedback and coaching to enhance EI skills, leading to more emotionally intelligent workplaces.

Focus on Empathetic Leadership: In the future, leadership will increasingly shift toward empathetic, people-focused approaches. Traditional command-and-control leadership styles are being replaced by leadership models that prioritize empathy, emotional connection, and collaboration. This shift reflects the growing recognition that emotionally intelligent leaders are more effective at inspiring and motivating teams, fostering innovation, and driving long-term success.
- Prediction: Empathetic leadership will become the norm in successful organizations, with leaders who prioritize emotional intelligence outperforming those who rely solely on authority or technical expertise.

Emotional Intelligence in Customer Experience (CX): As competition in the marketplace intensifies, organizations are recognizing the importance of emotional intelligence in delivering exceptional customer experiences. Emotionally intelligent employees are better able to understand customer emotions, anticipate their needs, and create positive interactions that build long-term loyalty.
- Prediction: Emotional intelligence will become a key differentiator in customer service and customer experience, with organizations prioritizing EI training for customer-facing roles to enhance the emotional connection with their clients.

The Future Workplace: Emotionally Intelligent Cultures
As emotional intelligence continues to gain prominence, it will have a profound impact on organizational cultures and business practices. Emotionally intelligent workplaces are characterized by open communication, trust, collaboration, and respect for individual emotions. These cultures foster psychological safety, where employees feel empowered to express themselves, take risks, and innovate without fear of judgment.

Creating Emotionally Intelligent Cultures: In the future, businesses will place a greater emphasis on building cultures where emotional intelligence is embedded into the fabric of the organization. This means not only hiring for EI but also promoting EI skills throughout the company by rewarding behaviors that demonstrate empathy, collaboration, and emotional regulation.
- Prediction: Emotionally intelligent cultures will become a competitive advantage, attracting top talent and fostering higher levels of employee engagement, retention, and innovation.

Psychological Safety as a Standard Practice: Psychological safety—the belief that you can speak up, take risks, and make mistakes without fear of retribution—will become a standard expectation in emotionally intelligent workplaces. Leaders who foster psychological safety will see increased creativity, innovation, and team collaboration, as employees feel safe to share their ideas and take initiative.

- Prediction: Organizations that prioritize psychological safety will be more agile, innovative, and able to adapt to changing market conditions, giving them a competitive edge.

Emotional Intelligence and Leadership Diversity: The future of business leadership will also see a greater emphasis on diversity in leadership roles. Emotional intelligence will be crucial in creating inclusive environments where diverse leaders can thrive. Leaders with high EI will be better able to navigate diverse perspectives, encourage open dialogue, and foster a sense of belonging across all levels of the organization.
- Prediction: Emotional intelligence will play a key role in promoting leadership diversity, with organizations that embrace diverse leadership styles and perspectives outperforming those that don't.

The Long-Term Impact of Emotional Intelligence on Business Success
The long-term impact of emotional intelligence on business success is profound. Organizations that invest in building emotional intelligence among their leaders and teams will enjoy several competitive advantages, including:

Stronger Employee Engagement and Retention: Emotionally intelligent leaders create environments where employees feel valued, supported, and motivated. This leads to higher levels of engagement and lower turnover, as employees are more likely to stay with organizations that prioritize their emotional well-being.
- Prediction: Companies that cultivate emotional intelligence will see increased employee retention and a more engaged, productive workforce.

Improved Team Collaboration and Innovation: Emotionally intelligent teams are more collaborative, creative, and innovative. By fostering a culture of open communication and trust, leaders with high EI enable their teams to work together more effectively, share ideas freely, and develop innovative solutions to complex problems.

Better Decision-Making and Problem-Solving: Emotionally intelligent leaders are better equipped to make informed, balanced decisions, as they can manage their emotions and consider both logical and emotional factors. This leads to better problem-solving and more strategic decision-making in high-pressure situations.

- Prediction: Businesses led by emotionally intelligent leaders will outperform those that rely solely on technical or analytical skills, as emotionally intelligent leaders make more nuanced and well-rounded decisions.

Conclusion: The Future of Emotional Intelligence in Business

As we look to the future, it's clear that emotional intelligence will continue to be a critical driver of business success. From leading remote teams to navigating diversity and inclusion, emotional intelligence is essential for managing the complexities of modern leadership and building organizations that are resilient, innovative, and people-centered.

Emotionally intelligent leaders will not only adapt to change—they will lead their teams through it, fostering cultures of trust, collaboration, and psychological safety. These leaders will be the ones who shape the future of business, ensuring that their organizations thrive in an increasingly dynamic and emotionally complex world.

As emotional intelligence continues to evolve and integrate with new technologies and workplace trends, it will remain one of the most valuable skills for leaders and teams alike. The future of business is emotional—and those who embrace emotional intelligence will lead the way.

www.ingramcontent.com/pod-product-compliance
Lightning Source LLC
Chambersburg PA
CBHW070401230526
45471CB00006B/2657